SIMON PETER

www.realreads.co.uk

Retold by Alan Moore and Gill Tavner
Illustrated by Karen Donnelly

Published by Real Reads Ltd
Stroud, Gloucestershire, UK
www.realreads.co.uk

ISBN 978-1-906230-26-5

Printed in China by Imago Ltd
Designed by Lucy Guenot
Typeset by Bookcraft Ltd, Stroud, Gloucestershire

CONTENTS

THE CHARACTERS

Simon Peter

Simon is a simple fisherman. What qualities does Jesus see in him? Can Simon learn enough from his weaknesses to be able to do the work that Jesus has in mind for him?

Jesus

Simon's love for Jesus is unlimited and unquestioning. What will Jesus demand of Simon? Will Simon ever let him down?

Judas

Judas is one of Jesus's twelve most trusted friends, but can Simon Peter also trust him completely?

Mary Magdalene

When Jesus heals Mary Magdalene, she becomes an important supporter of his work. What startling news will she bring to Simon Peter?

Pontius Pilate

Pilate is the Roman governor of the province. He offers to release a prisoner, but who will it be?

Stephen

Stephen proves himself a brave and virtuous man. Will Simon ever be as brave as him?

Paul

Paul is well known for persecuting Jesus's followers, but now claims to have changed his mind. Should Simon Peter trust him?

SIMON PETER

Catching fish. That's what Andrew and I were doing on the day that changed our lives for ever. That was what we had always done; it was what our father and our grandfather had always done. For generations we had lived as fishermen in the village of Capernaum, by the Sea of Galilee. Until that day, we had no expectation of ever doing anything else.

We were good Jews. We respected the Sabbath, Jewish festivals and Jewish laws. Until that day, we thought this was the way to satisfy God. How wrong we were. He wanted so much more.

The day started like any other. Having cast our nets into the lake, Andrew and I were beginning to relax, drifting just offshore. Waiting.

'Hey!' We looked up. A man was calling, and beckoning to us from the shore.

'Simon, who is that?' asked Andrew. 'Isn't it Jesus?'

I wasn't sure. It looked like Jesus, who we had seen a few times in town, but we were still quite far from the shore. We pulled in our nets, sailed back, and beached the boat.

Jesus looked at us. We looked at him. Though nobody spoke, we didn't feel awkward. I felt a great sense of peace, rather like the period immediately after casting the nets. It was Jesus who broke the silence. 'Come, leave your nets. I will make you fishers of people.'

We must have looked like caught fish ourselves as we stared at him open-mouthed. He seemed amused. 'Follow me,' he invited, turning away.

Looking back, it's hard to remember quite what made us decide to follow him, but we did. Just like that.

Jesus invited our neighbours, James and John, to follow him too. From that day we all stayed together. Jesus taught us and trusted us. Other people joined us. Eventually, from

the growing crowd, Jesus selected eight other
men to help him. We were from a range of
backgrounds – there were even tax collectors,
and one man, Judas, was the son of a priest. He
was better educated than most of us, as he often
liked to point out. Jesus entrusted Judas with
responsibility for our money.

There were many other followers, but Jesus relied upon us twelve.

We followed Jesus around Galilee. He taught in synagogues, by the lakeside, and on mountaintops – anywhere that people gathered. News of his preaching spread quickly, and he was soon attracting huge crowds. He made it clear that he had come to help the poor, the weak and the suffering. Looking back, I can see that it was so simple, but at the time I often misunderstood what he was telling us.

You may wonder why so many people wanted to hear Jesus. Well, some wanted to learn from him; others were simply curious. Many hoped that Jesus would lead a revolt against the Romans, or change the Jewish laws, the Torah. However, he insisted that he had come to fulfil the Torah rather than abolish it. Jesus taught that our love of God should show in how we treat other people, even the Romans. We should help the poor and the weak, and we should love and forgive our enemies. Jesus always closed with the same simple prayer, then sent his listeners to go and live in the way he had taught.

Sick people came to Jesus to be healed. He made lame people walk; he cured lepers; he even made dead people live again. In the early days, when we were still in Capernaum, he cured my mother-in-law of a fever.

On another occasion he healed a woman, Mary Magdalene, who was possessed by demons. After this, Mary committed herself to Jesus's work.

She was a wealthy woman, and her support was very useful to us. She sometimes joined us on our travels, which seemed strange at first, but I soon got used to her.

Jesus expected a great deal more of his twelve close followers than he expected of anybody else. One evening, he drew us together. 'I have work for you to do,' he said. 'There's too much for me alone. Go, preach my message, heal the sick. You now have God's authority.'

Perhaps we looked a little too pleased, because he warned us, 'People will hate you and try to kill you because of me.' This was frightening, but I have never forgotten his next words. 'Although they may hurt your body, if you stand firm to the end, they cannot kill your soul.'

The work was exhausting for us all, but especially for Jesus, who never stopped. Once, after a particularly busy day when we hadn't even had time to eat, Jesus appeared sad and weary. He gave us the news that John the Baptist, a holy man and Jesus's friend, had been beheaded by King Herod.

'I need time alone to pray,' Jesus told us.

We helped him into a boat on Galilee. Although we tried to do this discreetly, we couldn't stop the noisy crowds following him along the shore. Later that evening, we caught up with them. Jesus had left his boat and found a small hill on which to stand and teach. Although it was growing late, over five thousand men, women and children were still listening intently. They must all have been as hungry as we were.

Andrew nudged Jesus. 'We should let them go to the village for food.'

'No,' replied Jesus. 'Feed them here.' We looked at each other. We only had five loaves and two fish between us. This wouldn't feed us, let alone five thousand people.

'Do you really want me to go and spend two

hundred silver coins on bread for them all?' asked Judas, incredulous.

Jesus took a loaf. Looking up to heaven, he thanked God, broke the bread into pieces, and gave it to us to distribute. I looked at the basket and looked at the crowds. This wouldn't go very far!

I gave a small piece to a man, the same to another. Having anxiously fed a few people in this way, I began to notice that the food in my basket, rather than diminishing, was increasing. No matter how much food I took out, my basket always seemed to be full. I looked over at Thaddeus, who was feeding another group.

The same thing was happening there.

When the crowds had eventually dispersed, we found ourselves left with twelve baskets full of food. I sat next to Jesus. 'You knew, didn't you?'

Jesus was laughing. 'Help yourselves.'

That night, leaving Jesus to enjoy his longed-for solitude, the twelve of us took a boat out onto the lake. The water was calm, but the clouds threatened a storm. As an experienced fisherman, I offered to stay awake and keep an eye on the weather. The hours slipped slowly by, and the wind strengthened. As I stared sleepily across the water, I was chilled by an eerie vision. Something white, perhaps a spirit, was drifting towards us over the choppy water.

'Don't be afraid,' a voice called. 'It's me, Jesus.' Jesus reached out his hand to me. 'Come, Simon.'

I stepped gingerly out of the boat. I was walking on water. A miracle! But the mocking wind buffeted me. Walking on water? The wind howled with laughter. Impossible!

Doubt soaked through my clothes with the spray. I began to sink. 'Lord, save me!' I called.

Jesus reached out his hand and caught me. 'Oh, you of little faith.' He frowned. 'Why did you doubt?'

I had disappointed Jesus. It was frustrating. I always tried so hard, but I seemed to make more mistakes than the others. I needed more than my fair share of Jesus's patience.

Jesus told many short stories, or parables. Desperate to understand them, I often asked him to explain. I remember him once sighing wearily, 'Simon, do you still not understand?' But he always explained gently and kindly.

I still feel astonished that Jesus chose me, that amongst all his followers he decided that I should be the foundation for the future. We were in the region of Caesarea Philippi when it happened.

'Who do people say I am?' he asked us.

'Some say you are John the Baptist,' answered James, 'or a prophet.'

'Who do you say I am?' Jesus seemed to be looking at me.

'You are Christ, the son of the living God,' I answered.

Jesus nodded. 'Simon, you are blessed, because this was revealed to you by God. From now on I shall call you Peter, which means "rock". On this rock I will build my church and no evil shall overcome it. I will give you the keys of the kingdom of heaven, where you must show the same love and compassion that have been shown to you.'

Was he mocking me? I was probably the least rock-like person I had ever known. The others seemed as dumbfounded as I was. Jesus told us to sit down at the roadside. 'Do not tell anyone who I am,' he warned us. 'I must soon go to Jerusalem where I will be judged and put to death. Three days later I will rise from the dead.'

Horrified, appalled, I jumped up. 'No! No! That mustn't happen!'

Jesus looked at me sternly. 'Get behind me,

Satan! You are a stumbling block to me; you have in mind the things of men, not the things of God.'

I felt ashamed. Again.

Later I approached Jesus. 'How can I be a rock?'

'You love God. You love me.'

'But I make more mistakes than all of the others put together.'

'Because you try, you make mistakes. Because you make mistakes, you will grow.'

Several days later we were in the mountains. Jesus asked John, James and me to accompany him to the top of one of them. Hot and thirsty, we finally reached the summit. Jesus seemed to have something on his mind, and wandered away. We collapsed on the ground. Then the strangest thing happened. We watched in wonder as he became bathed in a strange light. His face and clothes shone like sunlight. Then two equally bright figures appeared beside him. They were Moses

and Elijah. I didn't know what to do. Trembling
with terror, I offered, 'Lord, we will make three
shelters – one for each of you.'

Jesus didn't respond. Then a cloud
enveloped the three of them, and a voice
rumbled all around us. 'This is my own dear
son – listen to him.'

We threw ourselves down in fear. Jesus came over and touched us gently, telling us not to be afraid. When we looked up, he was alone again.

It was hard to find the right words to talk about what had happened, so we descended the mountain in silence. Near the bottom, Jesus instructed us, 'Don't tell anyone what you have seen here until I have risen from the dead.'

In the following weeks, Jesus continued to refer to what lay ahead. He would be killed, he would rise again, and the kingdom of God would come. I don't think any of us really understood. I decided not to ask questions.

Jesus continued his work, whilst we still struggled to understand. One day, Judas asked, 'Master, who is the greatest in the kingdom of heaven?'

As so often, Jesus's answer sounded contradictory. 'Whoever wants to be first,' he replied, 'must place himself last and be the servant of all.' Some children were playing nearby. Jesus called one of them over to him. Crouching beside the boy, Jesus said, 'Whoever welcomes one of these children in my name welcomes me. Whoever welcomes me, welcomes God.'

On another occasion, some mothers asked Jesus to bless their babies. We were concerned that Jesus had done enough for one day, and started to usher them away. But Jesus stopped us. 'Bring the children to me. The kingdom of God belongs to such as these.' Tired though he was, he took the babies in his arms and blessed them.

I think I understood this time.

To him, children represented the powerless, the voiceless, those most in need of kindness and protection.

Jesus's preaching could be both simple and complex at the same time. I remember a young man who approached Jesus, and anxiously asked him, 'Teacher, what must I do to receive eternal life?'

'Obey the commandments,' was Jesus's simple answer.

'Which ones?'

'Do not murder; do not commit adultery; do not steal; do not lie; respect your father and mother; and love your neighbour as yourself.'

'Master,' the man said, 'I have kept these. What else must I do?'

Jesus looked at him with love. 'Give all your possessions to the poor. Then come and follow me.' The young man's face fell; from his clothes we could see that he was quite wealthy. He walked away, deep in thought.

Jesus turned to us. 'Everybody has something which blocks their relationship with God. For that young man, it is his riches. To enter the kingdom of God, you must put God first, over everything else.'

How did this apply to us? 'We have given up everything,' I said. 'What is our reward?'

'You will reign with God, showing the same love and compassion to others as you have been shown. Everybody who puts God first, even above home and family, will receive eternal life.' A fine promise, but still I was haunted by the future Jesus had foreseen for himself here on earth.

The time came to travel to Jerusalem. Some of our group thought that this might be the beginning of Jesus's challenge to the power of Herod and Rome. Perhaps we were going to set up a new government run on holy principles. I wasn't so sure. Jesus had already warned us that he was fulfilling the scriptures; that horrors lay ahead. I heard my friends' hopes, but I couldn't share them.

The journey took several days. As we wearily approached Jerusalem, Jesus sent James and John ahead to the next village. 'You will find a donkey tied up there. Tell the owner that the master needs it.' When they returned, we put our cloaks on the donkey's back and Jesus mounted. He led us into Jerusalem.

Just as is written in the scriptures, crowds lined the streets, shouting psalms of expectation and cheering. 'Hosanna in the highest! Blessed is he who comes in the name of the Lord!'

Many pulled down palm branches, which they waved or spread before us. The palm is a national emblem, a sign of patriotism. The crowd's emotional reaction must have made the authorities feel very nervous. Perhaps my friends were right. This could be the beginning of an uprising.

At night, we left the city and slept in a nearby village called Bethany. The next morning we returned to Jerusalem's temple. Jesus had been angry since we visited the temple the day before. Once there, he overturned a money-lender's table. Following Jesus's lead, we caused chaos, overturning tables and benches, and releasing animals destined for sacrifice. In the middle of the confusion, Jesus called out, 'It is written, "My house shall be called a house of prayer," but you have made it a den of thieves.'

We had made a bold statement and upset many people. Trouble lay ahead. The Romans would be nervous about a possible uprising. The temple authorities would see Jesus as a direct challenge.

Indeed, in the following days, whenever Jesus taught in the temple, the priests' anger was evident in their faces, but they were powerless to act against Jesus in front of so many people. A riot would threaten their own positions. I noticed Judas talking with one of the priests. Judas looked uncomfortable.

The period of Passover arrived, normally a time for celebration and thanksgiving. On the first day of the festival, Jesus sent us towards a particular part of the city. 'You will find a man with a room. Tell him to prepare his room; we will celebrate the Passover at his house.'

That evening, Jesus was unusually quiet. The mood at the dinner table was sombre, not the happy family atmosphere we used to have at home on these occasions. I asked Jesus what was wrong.

'One of you here will betray me.'

'Who?' asked John. We were all anxious to know who it could possibly be.

Jesus spoke over our noise. 'One who dips his hand in the bowl with me.'

I noticed a swift movement to Jesus's right. Was it Judas? Did he move his hand away from the bowl? 'Surely not I, Rabbi?' I heard him ask.

Jesus whispered something to him. Poor Judas turned pale. A few minutes later, he left the room.

Jesus picked up some bread, thanked God for it, and broke it into pieces. He gave each of us a piece. 'Take and eat, this is my body.' Then he picked up the cup of wine, gave thanks, and passed that around too. 'Drink this, all of you. This is my blood, God's new promise, poured out for many for the forgiveness of sins. I will never again drink this wine until I am in my father's kingdom.'

I exchanged glances with the rest of the group. Was the dreaded time so close at hand?

Later that evening, Jesus wanted to go to the Garden of Gethsemane, outside the city walls. I think he felt that there he would find the peace, and the strength, for prayer. It was already dark, but the moon was bright. The walk took us through the eerie tombs of the Kidron Valley, darkening our spirits further. As we walked, Jesus sighed. 'Tonight, you will all flee from me. After I am raised to life I will return to Galilee ahead of you.'

I felt hurt. 'I'll never leave you, master, even if the others do.'

'Peter,' Jesus sounded sad, 'before the cock crows tonight, you will deny three times that you know me.'

'I'll never deny you, even if I have to die with you,' I insisted. 'Never.'

Jesus didn't respond.

Jesus took just three of us into the garden with him. I looked closely at the face I loved so well.

I had never seen him so troubled. He asked us to keep watch while he went to pray. We tried, really we did, but when Jesus returned, he found us all asleep. 'Couldn't you stay awake with me for just one hour?' He seemed disappointed. 'I'll go again. Pray that you don't fall asleep this time. Your spirit is willing, but your flesh is weak.'

I fixed my eyes on Jesus. Sweat ran down his face as he prayed. We prayed too, as he had directed, but prayer lulled us back to sleep. Again, Jesus returned to find us sleeping. We were ashamed. This happened a third time, but when Jesus woke us this time he seemed at last to be at peace with himself. 'Are you still sleeping?' he smiled. 'Enough! The hour has come! Look, here is the man who betrays me.'

Judas arrived with armed men. 'Greetings, teacher,' he said, stepping forward and kissing Jesus.

Jesus looked directly at him. 'Friend, do what you came for.' Unbelievable! How could he call Judas 'friend'? They arrested Jesus. I prepared to fight, but Jesus stopped me. He turned to his captors. 'Why did you come with swords to capture me? I was with you in the temple every day and you did nothing.'

They took him away, a figure of calm in the chaos.

'Run!' urged Matthew. 'We'll regroup in Bethany.' I stayed. I had promised not to leave Jesus. I followed the soldiers to the house of Caiaphas, the high priest. Covering my head, I crept into the courtyard and sank into the shadows.

The priests challenged Jesus. 'Are you the son of God?'

He answered quietly, 'It is as you say.' They accused him of blasphemy and beat him. I knew that I would be in great danger if anybody recognised me as Jesus's friend. I was terrified, but I couldn't leave him. I hoped the darkness would hide me.

A serving-woman sidled close to me. 'Weren't you with Jesus of Galilee?' she whispered.

'I don't know what you're talking about,' I said, and moved away from her.

Then a girl, talking with others in a group, pointed to me. 'That man was with Jesus of Galilee!'

'I swear I don't know this man you're talking about.' I moved away again.

The group wouldn't leave me alone, and followed me. 'You are, you're one of his friends from Galilee,' another girl observed. 'You have a Galilean accent.'

Terrified, I shouted, 'I swear I don't know him! May God punish me if I lie!'

The tense silence following my outburst was broken by the crowing of a cock. I remembered Jesus's words. My tears of shame and grief tasted bitter.

Early the next morning, I learned that the Council of Priests had condemned Jesus to death and had handed him over to the Roman governor, Pontius Pilate. As I hurriedly joined the crowds outside the palace, Pilate appeared on the balcony. Behind him, his guards shoved Jesus and another prisoner.

Priests were slithering amongst the crowd, whispering venom. 'Jesus is a fraud,' they sneered. 'He said he was the messiah. He was going to liberate us Jews from the Romans. Now look at him!'

I looked. I wept inwardly. Brutally cut and bruised, Jesus looked exhausted.

Then Pilate addressed the crowd. 'Here is Jesus, who some of you call the anointed, and here is Barabbas, a murderer and thief. As it is your feast

of Passover,
I will release
a prisoner of
your choice.'

There was
a moment of quiet.
Here was hope. I held my breath. A man near me
shouted, 'Release Barabbas!'

I stood, appalled, as the crowd joined his chant.
I turned to the man. 'Why Barabbas?'

'He's a freedom fighter,' he replied, 'not like
this ineffective Jesus.' He turned back to face the
balcony. 'Crucify him!' he shouted.

This was insane! Pilate looked as perplexed as
I felt. 'Why?' he called. Receiving no reply other
than a crescendo of 'Crucify him,' Pilate washed his
hands and held them up to the crowd. 'This man's
blood is on your hands, not mine.'

Later that morning Roman soldiers nailed Jesus to a cross.

The moment Jesus died, the earth shook. Everything around us and everything within me shook. When stillness returned, the world was different. And so was I.

Jesus was dead. His followers were in great danger. I hurried through back streets to a friend's house. James and John were already there. Shocked and ashamed, we didn't know what to say to each other. I feared that all we had strived for over the last three years had failed. We didn't know that our work had only just begun.

We tried to observe the Sabbath, but our hearts were broken.

Word came that one of Jesus's followers, a man called Joseph of Aramethea, had taken Jesus's body and had placed it in his own tomb. We couldn't do anything about a proper burial on the Sabbath, but tomorrow we would attend to it. That night, the earth shook again.

Early the next morning, I was wakened by a loud banging at the door. Mary Magdalene was outside, shouting my name. 'His body has gone!' she gasped.

'What do you mean, gone?'

'The stone blocking the tomb has been rolled aside. We found an angel sitting on the stone. He said that Jesus has risen from the dead!' I shouted for the others while I fumbled to fasten my sandals.

'That's not all,' continued Mary. 'I saw Jesus. He spoke to me. He said he will meet you all in Galilee.'

'Are you sure he wants to meet me?' I asked, remembering my denial of him.

'He said all of you.'

'James! John!' I shouted, running from the door, elated. 'Follow me. Quickly!'

We ran to the tomb. John, a faster runner, got there first, but he hesitated at the entrance.

When I arrived, panting, I brushed past John and went straight in. Mary was right. Jesus's body wasn't there. The cloth in which he had been wrapped was discarded, as if the body inside had simply melted away.

That evening I sent a message to the others in Bethany. They arrived in twos and threes. Only Thomas was missing. 'Lock the doors,' I told James. A strange calm descended. I looked up and saw Jesus in our midst. We fell down in awe and joy and worshipped him.

'Peace be with you,' said Jesus. 'As my father sent me as a teacher, so I send you. Teach people that I died for them. Tell them to trust me and to follow me. Be sure of this – I am with you always.'

We returned to Galilee. It was safer than Jerusalem. Over the next forty days Jesus appeared to us several times. One night, some of us were out on the lake, fishing. At dawn, disappointed with our empty nets, we headed back to shore.

'Have you caught anything?' called a man from the shore.

'Not a thing.'

'Cast your nets on the other side of the boat.'

We did as the man said. The nets were immediately filled with so many fish that we had difficulty pulling them in.

I realised who the man was.

'Jesus!' I cried, plunging into the water to swim to him. He had lit a fire, on which he was already cooking fish. He had bread too, which he broke in his familiar way and shared with us.

After our meal, Jesus asked me, 'Do you love me?'

'Yes Lord. You know that I love you.'

'Feed my sheep,' he commanded. I understood that he meant I should teach the people.

Later he asked me again, 'Do you love me?' and again I said I did.

Again he said, 'Feed my sheep.'

A third time he asked me. It reminded me of the three times I had denied knowing him. Sadly, I said, 'Lord, you know everything. You know that I love you.'

'Feed my sheep.' Then I understood. He had forgiven my denials of him. He spoke again. 'Peter, when you are old they will stretch out your hands, bind you, and take you to a place that you don't want to go to.'

This shocked me. He seemed to be saying that I would die in the same way he had died. It has taken me a long time to accept that this will be my eventual end. Meanwhile I have God's work to do.

The last time we saw Jesus, he again urged us to continue his work down here on earth. 'You will be filled with God's power,' he told us. 'John baptised people with water, but you will be baptised with the Holy Spirit.' He looked up, and started to rise from the ground – we watched in amazement as he slowly ascended, and continued watching until the clouds hid him from our view.

Then began a period of waiting.

The eleven of us remaining since Judas left met frequently to pray as a group, along with Mary Magdalene and Jesus's mother. Other believers joined us until we numbered over one hundred. We elected Matthias to take Judas's place.

As Jesus had promised, we were visited by the Holy Spirit. One day, we were all gathered together when a noise like a strong wind filled the house. We felt as though tongues of fire from heaven ignited us with the ability to speak in languages we had never spoken before. People from outside, hearing the noise, came to see what had happened. There were people from many countries. Each of them heard us in their own language. They were amazed.

The power of the Holy Spirit spoke through me to the crowds. 'God sent Jesus to be handed over to his enemies who crucified him. God raised Jesus from the dead. Jesus is Lord and Christ.'

I called on them to turn away from sin and be baptised. About three thousand people were baptised and joined us that day. Our numbers continued to grow, and many joined us in teaching, spreading the word of Jesus.

Some time later, a lame man begged money from me as I entered a temple with John.

'I have neither food nor money,' I replied, 'but I will give you what I have. In the name of Jesus Christ, get up and walk.' I helped him to stand, and he walked with us into the temple. Recognising him as the lame beggar, people were amazed.

'Why are you surprised?' I asked. 'We have done this in Jesus's name.' Many who heard me believed, but the temple guards were angry and arrested us.

The next day they took us before the priests who had helped to condemn Jesus. 'How did you heal the beggar?' they demanded.

We told them about Jesus and about the gift of the Holy Spirit. After discussing the matter in whispers, they warned us never again to speak about Jesus or teach in his name.

'Which is right, to obey you or to obey God?' I asked. 'We must speak of what we have seen and heard.'

Unsure what to do, and unable to deny that the lame man could now walk, they repeated their warning and set us free.

There were now about five thousand of us teaching about Jesus. The temple authorities felt increasingly threatened. Once again, they arrested some of us. That night an angel opened our prison doors. 'Go to the temple courts and teach,' he told us.

We did as he said. When the guards found us, we were surrounded by crowds. The guards led us quietly out. Once again I found myself standing before the council of priests. They were angry because we had ignored their warnings.

'We must obey God, not people,' I explained calmly.

'These people are trouble. We should kill them,' someone murmured.

A wise council member called Gamaliel advised the council to release us. 'If their purpose is of human origin, these people will fail,' he told them, 'but if their purpose is from God as they claim, you will find yourselves fighting against God: you will not win.'

Thanks to Gamaliel, we were whipped rather than killed. Although it was agonising, we felt honoured to suffer in God's name.

By now there were so many believers in Jesus that the twelve of us found them hard to manage. An unpleasant disagreement arose between two groups of believers about the distribution of food. I suggested that they should choose seven people to look after the believers' business affairs, which would leave us free to concentrate on preaching.

One of the men chosen was Stephen. He was a man richly blessed by God, and his face shone with virtue, but I think some people were jealous of his position. They bribed others to lie to the council that they had heard Stephen say that Jesus would destroy Jerusalem and change the law of Moses.

Stephen was accused of blasphemy, and summoned to appear before the council.

A friend who attended the trial told me that he spoke eloquently and at great length. 'Was there ever a prophet that you and your fathers did not persecute?' he challenged them. 'They even killed those who predicted the coming of Jesus. And now you have betrayed and murdered Jesus, who was the best of us all. You have received the law from angels, but have not obeyed it.'

What courage! Stephen must have known that this would anger the council. Of course, they were furious, but Stephen looked up to heaven and saw the glory of God. 'I see heaven,' he said, 'with Jesus standing at the right hand of God.'

The council members, now furious, dragged Stephen outside and pushed him over the edge of a cliff. The crowd threw rocks down on him. As the great stones broke his body, Stephen prayed for God to forgive those who threw them.

I mourned the loss of a good man, a good friend. Will I have such courage when my time comes?

Stephen's death marked the beginning of the persecution of the followers of Jesus in Jerusalem. A man named Saul was particularly influential in persecuting us. He was responsible for many cruel deaths.

We fled, travelling far and wide. We taught and healed wherever we went, spreading the good news that Jesus had died in order to show us a new way to God. One day, having secretly met up in Jerusalem, we heard strange news from Damascus. Saul, our main persecutor, was claiming to have seen the risen Christ. He was bravely preaching Jesus's message, and had changed his name to Paul.

Can we trust him? we wondered.

Paul's preaching eventually brought him to Jerusalem. He was looking for us. Was this a trick? Could we trust him?

'He has preached fearlessly in Jesus's name,' argued Barnabas. 'We must welcome him.'

I felt my old uncertainty return. I wished that Jesus was there to tell me what to do. I decided that I had to trust God. When Paul knocked on our door, I opened it

wide. 'Welcome, Paul.' My trust was rewarded. Paul became a good friend and ally.

With Paul on our side, our lives became safer. I continued to travel. One afternoon, in Joppa, I had gone onto a flat roof to find quiet and to pray. In my prayer, I saw a vision in which a sheet was lowered from heaven, containing all kinds of animals, reptiles and birds – creatures we would not normally eat. Then a voice said, 'Get up, Peter. Kill and eat.'

'Surely not, Lord!' I replied, 'I have never eaten anything impure or unclean.'

The voice answered, 'Do not call anything impure that God has declared clean.'

This happened three times in all. Then the voice said, 'Now, Peter, three men are waiting for you downstairs. Go with them.'

I went downstairs. The men worked for a Roman centurion called Cornelius, who had

told them to bring me to him. We left the next morning. When we reached his house, Cornelius knelt at my feet. I felt embarrassed. 'Get up. I am only a man, like you,' I said. I now understood the meaning of my vision.

I explained to Cornelius, 'By our law, a Jew is not allowed to associate with non-Jews, but God has shown me that Jesus and his teaching are for all people.' We talked about Jesus's life and death and about his teachings. Everything was now clear to me. I agreed to baptise these men, even though they were Romans.

When I returned to Jerusalem my friends criticised my actions, but when I described my vision, they praised God. 'Peter, you were right

to give Romans the opportunity to repent and turn
to Jesus,' said Philip.

King Herod, the ruler of Judea, was becoming
nervous of our growing influence. He might be
Jewish, but he worked for the Romans, and wanted
to please them. He began another persecution.

First James was tried and executed, and then
I was arrested again. I was heavily guarded and
chained. One night, in a dream, an angel came to
me. 'Get up and follow me,' he said. My chains
fell off, the prison gate opened,
and I walked past the guards.
When I woke up, I really
was free. Wrapping my cloak
around my face to avoid recognition, I hurried
to a house in which many of my friends were
gathered. I knocked softly until they let me in.
I told them what had happened, and then fled.
Herod's men would soon come looking for me.

Inside, I am still Simon the fisherman. Although Jesus named me Peter and gave me strength, purpose and understanding, I still experience my old uncertainties. I've now spent half of my life teaching, healing, and fleeing persecution. I'm growing weary, but my work is not finished.

There are divisions amongst our people. They argue over how freely we can reinterpret Jewish law. I don't know the answer, but others have strong opinions. Worried, I travel and talk to various groups. 'Discuss calmly,' I urge, 'respect each other's opinions.' As often happens with anyone trying to keep the peace, I seem to attract anger from both sides.

The number of believers continues to increase. Paul has sent news that there are even believers in Rome. He has done well. He is a fearless preacher. However, not all news from Rome is good. Believers there are being persecuted for refusing to worship the Emperor as a god. Our believers in Rome have asked for our support.

'Peter, you should go,' my friends insisted yesterday. 'You are the most experienced. You knew Jesus best.'

'I am tired,' I replied. 'Choose a younger man instead.'

Yesterday I thought this was the right decision. Today is different.

Last night I dreamed that I was running away from Rome, frightened. I saw Jesus, hurrying in the opposite direction, towards Rome. I called out to him, 'Lord, where are you going?'

Without stopping he called back, 'Since you are leaving my sheep, I am going to Rome to be crucified again in your place.'

I stopped. Still in my dream, I turned round and began to walk back to Rome.

Now I know I must go to Rome. Although I am certain I am travelling towards the death that Jesus once predicted for me, I will not deny him this time. I am not afraid.

TAKING THINGS FURTHER
The real read

This *Real Reads* volume of *Simon Peter* is our interpretation of the events of the New Testament, told from the perspective of one of the most important participants. In writing this account of Simon Peter's life, we have used evidence from both the gospel according to Matthew and Acts of the Apostles. Matthew's gospel is one of the four gospels – the first four books of the New Testament.

It is important to acknowledge that all four of the gospels were written after Jesus's death, and that the writers had different aims in mind – although they all wanted to engender faith in the reader that Jesus was the Son of God. The first three gospels – Matthew, Mark and Luke – are called 'the synoptic gospels'. They were probably written between forty and sixty years after the crucifixion. The gospel according to John, written later, is significantly different.

Sometimes, the four gospels' accounts of events differ considerably. At first this made our task rather difficult, until we realised that what we needed to do was present the New Testament as it is, rather than to weave a path of our choice between the gospels. Therefore, if you read all six books in the *Real Reads* New Testament series, you may well notice some of the apparent contradictions and inconsistencies that are present in the Bible itself.

For the latter part of Simon Peter's life, we have drawn on evidence from Acts of the Apostles. Many people think Acts was written by the same Luke who wrote Luke's gospel, some time between 60 and 70 CE. The writer probably knew both Simon Peter and Paul.

Simon Peter did not write down his own thoughts and experiences, so we do not know what he thought of the events through which he lived. Using thorough research and paying close attention to the Bible account, we have tried to imagine what he might have been like, and what he might have thought.

This *Real Reads Simon Peter* does not cover all the events of the New Testament. Reading the other five books in the series will bring you closer to an understanding of the complete story. You may then want to read the New Testament itself. We recommend that you read either the *New International Version* or *The Youth Bible*, details of which are given below.

Biblical sources

On the *Real Reads* website you will find an online concordance (www.realreads.co.uk/ newtestament/concordance/simonpeter). A 'bible concordance' is an indexing tool which allows you to see how the same words, sentences and passages appear in different versions and translations of the Bible. This online concordance will direct you from events in the *Real Reads* version back to their biblical sources, so you can see clearly where each part of our story is drawn from. Although *Simon Peter* is based on the story as told in the gospel of Matthew and Acts, there are a few places where we have drawn on other sources.

Life in
New Testament times

The main events of Simon Peter's life with Jesus took place in Palestine, a long narrow area of land bordered to the west by the Mediterranean Sea and to the east by the Transjordanian Desert. Some parts of Palestine were desert, some were hill country, some rich pasture land, and some uncultivated wilderness.

Although Palestine was Jewish land, it was part of the Roman Empire and under Roman control. The Jews resented paying taxes to Rome. During Simon Peter's lifetime, there was considerable conflict between the Jews and their Roman rulers. This helps to explain why the Romans might have been nervous of the crowds following Jesus.

The Jews considered Palestine to be their 'promised land', promised to them by God. Moses had led them there from slavery in Egypt. The area was mainly Jewish, with synagogues and temples. Nevertheless, it is interesting that

most of Jesus's ministry took place around the Sea of Galilee, an area with a mixed population of Jews and Gentiles, and a reputation for political unrest. This is the area in which Simon Peter and his brother Andrew grew up.

Simon Peter lived in Capernaum, on the shores of the Sea of Galilee. Capernaum was a fishing town and a thriving commercial centre. Before he followed Jesus, Simon Peter had a secure living as a fisherman. During Jesus's ministry, the disciples based themselves in Capernaum, probably in Simon Peter's home. After Jesus's death, Simon Peter travelled widely and became a leader of the emerging Christian church.

Like most people, Simon Peter would have lived in a quite basic house built of mud or stone. The routines of people's lives followed the seasons as many were involved in agriculture, herding goats and sheep, or fishing. The area around the lake was quite fertile, growing a range of fruit, grain and vegetables. Fish and bread were staples of their diet.

Simon Peter was Jewish. Jews of the time, as is still the case for many orthodox Jews today, followed very strict laws. The Old Testament tells the story of how these laws, the Torah, were handed down from God to Moses. It must have been strange for Simon Peter when Jesus seemed to challenge the Torah.

Finding out more

We recommend the following books and websites to gain a greater understanding of the New Testament.

Books

We strongly recommend that you read the rest of the *Real Reads* New Testament series, as the six narratives interlock to give a more complete picture of events. These are *Jesus of Nazareth*, *Mary of Galilee*, *Judas Iscariot*, *Mary Magdalene* and *Paul of Tarsus*.

- *New Century Youth Bible*, Authentic Lifestyle, 2007.

- *Simon Peter: The Training Years* and *Simon Peter: Challenging Times*, Helen Clark, Day One Publications (Pocket Bible People), 2009.

- *People in the Life of Jesus*, Colin Lumsden, Day One Publications, 2003.

Websites

- www.bbc.co.uk/religion/religions/christianity
Lots of information about Jesus, history and the
Christian faith.

- www.localhistories.org/new.html
Brief but useful descriptions of many aspects of
everyday life in New Testament times.

- www.biblepath.com/peter
Brief but very accessible information to Simon Peter.

TV and film

- *Jesus of Nazareth* (1977), directed by Franco
Zeffirelli. ITV DVD. A six-and-a-half-hour mini
series.

- *The Miracle Maker* (2000), directed by Hayes,
Sokolov. ICON Home Entertainment. Animation.

- *The Parables of Jesus* (2006), Boulevard
Entertainment.

- *He is Risen* (2006), Boulevard Entertainment.
A 30-minute animation about the resurrection and
the meaning of Easter.

Food for thought

Here are some things to think about if you are reading *Simon Peter* alone, and ideas for discussion if you are reading it with friends.

Starting points

●   Simon Peter doesn't hesitate when Jesus asks him to follow. Why do you think this is? How do you think this fits with the often-heard advice not to follow strangers?

●   Simon Peter asks many questions. Write a list of his questions and the answers he receives.

●   Simon Peter makes many mistakes. Can you find some of them? Why do you think Jesus chooses him to be his 'rock'? What qualities do you think Jesus recognises in him?

●   On several occasions, Jesus tells people to serve others. Can you find some of these?

●   Why do you think Simon Peter denies knowing Jesus? How does he feel about this afterwards?

- Can you find evidence that Simon Peter begins to take on a leadership role immediately after Jesus's death?

- What change occurs in Simon Peter when the Holy Spirit enters him? Can you remember any times when you have suddenly gained confidence?

Group activities

- With a group of friends, choose some important scenes from the book and act them out. What advice would you give to the person playing Simon Peter?

- Talk to your friends about times when you have made mistakes. What did you learn from your mistakes? What do you think Jesus feels about Simon Peter's mistakes?

- Talk about friendship together. Draw up a list of qualities you look for in a friend. How many of these qualities does Simon Peter possess?